Name_____

CLASS EMAIL ADDRESS_____

PASSWORD_____

Beyond Computer Basics for Seniors

A DR. KATIE CANTY

COMPUTER TRAINING

BOOK 2

<u>Large Print Edition</u>

Some Prior Computer Experience Helpful

Very easy, fun, friendly learning activities

Welcome Beyond Computer Basics Participant

Fill This in First

My full name is _____

Start date_____

Completion date_____

Name of professor <u>Dr. Katie Canty</u>
<u>seniortechacademy@yahoo.com</u>

Senior Center location _____

My email address is _____

My password_____
  Each student has a class email address. Check inside your course folder.

Your goal(s)

What do you plan to use your computer skills for upon completion of this course?

_____

Your question(s)

Do you have a special question about computers, this class, or a suggestion? If so, write it here.

MISSION STATEMENT

The mission and vision of this course is development and demonstration of basic, intermediate, or advance computer literacy skills by 100% of course completers.

The goal is to equip senior citizens with up-to-date, useful computer technology training. Every class, depending upon needs, skill level, plus interests of students is different. Help us to achieve our mission by coming to class(es) and letting others know about classes. Contact your local senior center or retirement facility administrator to enroll. Dr. Canty can be contacted at seniortechacademy@yahoo.com.

There are 7 workshops to choose from. We usually cover about 2 to 3 workshops a month. Computer classes meet one morning a week for about two hours. New classes start every month. Enjoy our continuously up-dated computer classes for seniors. WELCOME.

WEEKLY COURSE SCHEDULE

PART ONE

Week 1-3: Workshop 1

Week 4-6: Workshops 2

Week 7-8: Workshops 3

PART TWO

Week 1-3: Workshop 4

Week 4-6: Workshops 5

Week 7-8: Workshops 6-7

OMG (OH MY GOSH) ACTIVITIES

- Hat Day
- Sports Day
- WIT Day (What Is IT?)
- Field Trip Day
- Class Newsletter
- Newest Tech Gadgets and Trends

CLASS PROCEDURES AND TIME FRAME

- Cell phones on silent or vibrate before training class begins
- Scheduled break(s)
- Food/beverage consumption allowed outside training area
- Restroom facilities used on an as-needed basis

1. Previous week chapter review and posttest	15 minutes
2. Current week show, tell, explain, discuss, Q&A	35 minutes
BREAK TIME	10 minutes
3. Individual student lab work completion	35 minutes
4. Preview of upcoming week's activities	5 minutes

CONTENTS

SYLLABUS
Beyond Computer Basics Participants
PART ONE 8 CLASS MEETINGS   PART TWO 8 CLASS MEETINGS

PROFESSOR
Dr. Katie Canty, Ed. D.
Certified Microsoft Office Specialist, Word

TELEPHONE (communication by email preferred)
EMAIL
seniortechacademy@yahoo.com
COMMUNICATION
There are 2 methods you can use to contact your instructor:
• Email message
• Cell/telephone (Leave a clear message with a call-back number.)

INSTRUCTIONAL METHODS
Instructional methods consist of lecture, discussion, question and answer, show and tell, research, hands-on individual lab work, group work, student and team presentations.

GOAL
One hundred per cent of course completers should demonstrate an ability to use a computer to digitally communicate using basic computer literacy skills and/or knowledge.

PERFORMANCE OBJECTIVES AND EXPECTATIONS
There are three things that each participant is expected to demonstrate upon completion of all training activities:

1. become more knowledgeable of how to use a computer, scanner, and printer to begin or to complete a digital photo communications project
2. use the Internet to get desired information from a website
3. begin a useful computer project related to a training lesson(s)

COURSE DESCRIPTION
CLASS HOURS: 16
PREREQUISITES: Some computer experience helpful
Communicate online with your pictures. Discover how easy it is to create, customize, and to share your old and new pictures. Learn how to scan and to post photos to email and to social websites. Create your own photo story calendar, website, eBook, or video. Learn more about marketing crafts and items online.

TEXTBOOK: *BEYOND COMPUTER BASICS FOR SENIORS* by Dr. Canty
SUGGESTED SOFTWARE: *USB* flash drive

COMMENT ON INTERNET ACCESS
Do you want or need access to a computer for practice? Use a senior center computer for practice. The county library or community college will have computers for you to use, too.

ATTENDANCE
Students should be in attendance a minimum of 80% or more of the scheduled class hours.

GRADES
A course completion document will be issued to academy course completers, preferably during the academy celebration ceremony.

WORKSHOP 1   DIGITAL IMAGES/PHOTOS
Goal: Convert Hard Copy Pictures To Digital Images

Objectives

1. Understand some basic digital photo editing terminology.

2. Use a scanner to convert some of your photo hard copy pictures to digital images.

Requests

➢ If you have a **digital camera** _with the cable_ or your mobile camera device _with instructions_, **bring it to class**.

➢ **Bring 4-6 old hard copy pictures** to practice scanning and editing.

Yes, I am Rev. Aaron Moore, age 89 at the time that I graduated with highest honor from the VERY FIRST computer academy.

WORKSHOP 1   PICTURES
BASIC PHOTO SCANNING TERMINOLOGY

1. **Digital** – a processing technique used by computers

2. **Flatbed scanner** – an electronic device that generates a digital representation of an image

3. **Flash Drive or USB** – a small storage device that can be used to transport files from one computer to another

4. **JPEG** – a computer file format for compression and storage of photographic digital images

5. **Save As/Save** – Save stores data back to the file folder it originally came from whereas "Save As" lets the user make a copy of the file in a different folder or make a copy with a different name.

6. **Attachment** – a document, picture, or file usually accompanying a message or related main document

7. **Crop** – to cut out or trim unneeded portions of an image or a page is to crop

8. **Cut** – to remove or take out **a section or** piece; like using electronic scissors to remove something

9. **Paste** – to insert a section or piece that was cut; like using scissors to cut something and then pasting it elsewhere

10.   **Drag and Drop** – to select, to carry, and to place a section or piece from one place to another in document or file

WORKSHOP 1   PICTURES
How do I scan my hard copy photos to digital images?

Scanning is an easy and very fun way to store and organize your pictures digitally and even to digitally share with friends and family. You need access to a computer, a scanner, and the software that comes pre-packaged with your scanner.

Read The Scanning Guidelines, First
If you have never used a flatbed scanner before, the tips at this address will help. Go to www.scantips.com. Read the information that relates to how to scan.

Give Scanning A Try, Practice Scanning One of Your Photos

1. Go ahead and clean the scanner's glass with an eye-glass like lint-free cloth. Wipe clean before and after each scan.

2. To scan a photo, place your photo face down on the glass. Avoid smudging the scanner glass.

3. Open your photo scanner software, look for the picture/photo/camera feature and select the Auto Mode.

4. Click the Scan link.

5. Use the preview feature to see what the finished scan will look like; if you don't like it, you can delete that image and scan the photo again after repositioning it.

6. Photos can be scanned to software packages for brightening, darkening, resizing, cropping. It's like applying makeup for enhancement to a scanned photo. The names of some photo editing software packages include: Microsoft Paint and Microsoft Office Picture Manager.

7. VERY IMPORTANT: **Put in your flash drive.** When your picture looks like you want, look to the top of the screen. Click on File, Save As. Use the command **SAVE AS, browse to find the removable flash drive designation, if using a computer or scanner in a public facility**. Saving as a JPEG file will work just fine for class purposes. If you do not have a flash drive, SAVE the scanned photo and email it to yourself as an attachment. When the scan wizard asks where to save the scanned photo, select the removable USB hard drive designation.

WORKSHOP 1   PHOTO SCANNING PRACTICE

SCAN ONE OF YOUR PHOTOS TO YOUR USB DRIVE FOR LATER USE

1. Select one of your photos to scan.

2. Scan the photo.

3. Name your scan: Example-- like Muffy's first birthday photo.

4. Save the scan to your USB drive as a JPEG file.

Look and find the saved scan on your USB drive, before removing your flash drive, also known as USB drive. Write down the name the name and extension showing on your USB drive for the picture that you scanned.   _____

WORKSHOP 1   COMPLETE SELF TEST 1

_____1. WHICH OF THESE IS A FILE EXTENSION?

A. carteretcounty.gov

B. mypicnicflyer.doc

C. unitedway.org

D. myfirstscan.jepg

E. all of the above

F. none of the above

_____2. OF THE FOLLOWING STATEMENTS, WHICH IS ACCURATE?

A. Scanners can only scan color photos.

B. Many scanners are also fax and copy machines.

C. Place the photo to be scanned face down on the glass.

D. Using the scan wizard really helps.

E. all of the above

F. none of the above

_____3. WHAT IS THE PURPOSE OF A USB DRIVE?

A. To scan photos

B. To send email messages

C. To make digital images

D. all of the above

F. none of the above

_____4. WHICH STATEMENT IS TRUE?

A. Save is not the same thing as Save As.

B. Documents do not have to have a name keyed in order to SAVE.

C. Once a document is scanned, it's too late to readjust it again.

D. Scanners can only scan color photos.

E. all of the above

MAKE YOUR OWN PHOTO STORY CALENDAR
SEND SOMEONE A PRESENT:
A PHOTOSTORY GREETING CARD CALENDAR

Want a different kind of greeting card? Create a photo story calendar greeting card using Word and 4 photos from your albums, or use online clipart and photos. Select or take 4 photos that relate to one theme like Mom's perfect vacation, Dad's pets, My hobbies, Family reunion children, etc. Print your completed photo story greeting card calendar and place it on the fridge door for your special someone(s) to view and enjoy.

Let's get started. Go to udemy.com and locate the search browse box. Key in Dr. Canty. Select the photo story greeting calendar course link. This site may require registration.

Let's Practice Making & Printing Your Photo Story Calendar

STEP 1

DECIDE ON YOUR CALENDAR THEME. Select just one theme. Theme examples include pets, babies, events, vacations, weddings, graduation, hobbies, adventures.

Where to get 4 photos/pictures?

- Old photo albums
- Cell phone
- Digital Camera
- Free online clip art and photos

STEP 2

1. SCAN AND SAVE PICTURES from your albums to your USB as JPEG files. **_OR_**

2. BROWSE THE INTERNET FOR CLIP ART AND PHOTOS that relate to one theme of your choosing. Save the pictures that you select from the clip art or Internet pictures as a JPEG file on your USB drive. If using Internet photos, be sure to use only Internet clipart and photos that specify free to the public.

STEP 3

1. Open Word.
2. Click on File, New, Calendars, current year Calendars.
3. Look at Available Templates and select the template named (current year) One page Family Photo Calendar.
4. Press any key to remove the message about replacing photos. In this space key a personal to and from message like: HAPPY MOTHER'S DAY NANA LILY FROM JO, ASIA, LITTLE LONDON.
5. Replace the photos with your photo selections.
6. Save as a PDF.

7. Print 1 copy.

COMMUNICATING WITH DIGITAL IMAGES

Accurately respond by identifying each statement as True or False.

_____1. A Facebook account requires a login name and password.

_____2. This is a URL address udemy.com.

_____3. Pictures and documents can be saved to a US drive.

_____4. The acronym or initials JPEG represents the file extension for pictures/photos.

_____5. To upload a picture from clipart or the Internet into a Word document, click on the word Insert at the top of the screen.

_____6. This is a correctly formatted email address: seniortechacademy.com.

_____7. The icon that usually represents an email attachment is the word Enclose or Attachment.

_____8. Most scanners are combination copiers and fax machines as well as scanning machines.

_____9. Lay the picture face up, then proceed to scan.

_____10. A place on the USB or other storage area must be specified in order to save a scanned photo for later use.

WORKSHOP 2   ATTACHMENTS
Goal: Email Attach Pictures or Documents

Objectives

1. Compose and send an email with a picture attachment.

2. Open an attachment that was emailed to you.

I am the 92 year old Marine Corps veteran that is mentioned in our computer academy theme song. I can digitally communicate now.

Want a copy of our Computer Academy theme song? Send an email with Theme Song in the subject line to Professor Canty at seniortechacademy@yahoo.com.

WORKSHOP 2   ATTACHMENTS
EMAIL ATTACHMENTS TERMINOLOGY

1. **Paper Clip Icon** – click to open or to send an attachment

2. **Selfie** – picture you take of yourself

3. **Open** – to view; like unfolding a letter to read it

4. **Download** – move data, software, information, files, etc. from a distant computer to yours

5. **Email Etiquette** – principles of respectful behavior that one should use when writing or answering email messages

6. **Security**– things that one can do to protect oneself from online viruses, harassment, threats and identity theft

7. **Email Emoticons** – a digital icon or a sequence of keyboard symbols that serves to represent a facial expression, such as :- for a smiling face

8. **Post** – insert pictures, make comments, key in questions, write something at a website for information or interactivity

9. **Bookmark** – saving the location of a webpage by clicking on your computer bookmark button so that you can go back to the webpage later more quickly

10. **Spam** – unsolicited bulk mail, can be nuisance e-mail from people and companies you have never heard of trying to sell you something online

WORKSHOP 2   OPENING ATTACHMENTS
How do I open an email attachment sent to me?
OPEN AN EMAIL ATTACHMENT
Got A Paper Clip/Attachment Symbol
By the Email Message?

To open an **attachment**, click on the icon that looks like a paper clip. **A paper clip with a file name by it means that someone has sent you an attachment** with the email message. It is like someone sending you a letter with other things accompanying the letter like a flyer or a check. Email is now the letter and attachments are like the flyer and/or check.

Some computers have software that checks the attachment to see if it is safe to open, or free of **viruses**. A virus is a program or piece of code that is unknowingly spread from one computer to another and interferes with a computer's operation. This is why some computer users open just the attachment(s) when they recognize the name of the sender, like emails and attachments from your professor. Photos and instructional documents are the most frequent email attachments in the senior center academy class emails.

Workshop 2 *OPENING* An Attachment Practice

1. Log into your class email account.

2. Open the email from Professor Canty that has Class Photo in the subject line.

3. Click on the paper clip to open. Choose download attachment.

4. Save to your USB by clicking File, Save As.

5. Give the attachment class photo a name like computer class picture.

6. Select the removable drive name to save it to.

7. Click Save.

WORKSHOP 2 *SENDING* An Attachment Practice
How do I send this photo along with my email message?

For this practice, take a new selfie today. Compose an email message to yourself and attach your new selfie.

1. After taking your selfie, save it to your USB with the word selfie and your first name like, selfiemickey.

2. Open your class email account.

2. Click on Compose.

3. Key in your email address.

4. Click Cc to also send a copy to seniortechacademy@yahoo.com.

5. Put My Newest Class Selfie in the subject line.

6. Click in the message box. Key these words--See your selfie.

7. Click on the paper clip icon.

8. When the attach file dialogue box opens,

WORKSHOP 2   EMAIL ATTACHMENT PROJECT
COMPUTER ACADEMY THEME SONG

Yes, we actually have a computer academy theme song. Avon Walker, a computer academy honor graduate, holds the rights as the author and composer.

Step 1: For this project, send an email with Theme Song Request in the subject line to seniortechacademy@yahoo.com. Ask for a copy of the theme song.

Step 2: In response to your request, a copy will be sent to you as an email attachment.

Step 3: Open the song attachment by clicking on the paper clip icon. Download and save it to your flash drive.

Step 4: Print a hard copy and place it in your class folder.

Step 5: Save a copy to your flash drive.

WORKSHOP 2	COMPLETE THIS SELF TEST

EMAIL ATTACHMENTS

Circle T if the statement is True. Circle F if the statement is False.

T F 1. All email attachments should be opened and saved to your flash drive.

T F 2. If you get an email from a stranded relative who wants you to send money right away, send the money immediately as this could be a real emergency.

T F 3. Click on the cell phone icon to open an attachment.

T F 4. When in the computer lab, click on SAVE AS to save a picture to your USB flash drive.

T F 5. Emails should include a topic in the email's subject line.

T F 6. If you win the lottery, email your friends, relatives, and enemies, too, a message about your plans for a new spouse, new address, and new everything.

T F 7. The procedure for opening a document attachment like a song is very different from the procedure for opening a photo attachment like a selfie.

Number correctly answered:
_____ out of 7

WORKSHOP 3   SOCIAL NETWORKS
Goal: To Post Pictures and Messages To Family & Friends

Objectives

1. Register and/or sign in at a social network website.

2. Post a pictures(s) and a message(s) to a social website.

3. Find and message a friend, relative, group, or business on a social website.

**Our Beyond Computer Basics
Social Network
and Email**

Facebook: beyond computerbasics

Email: beyondcomputerbasics@yahoo.com

WORKSHOP 3   SOCIAL NETWORKS
BASIC SOCIAL NETWORKING TERMINOLOGY

Social Network: a website like Facebook, Twitter, Reddit, and many others that enables users to communicate with each other by posting information, comments, messages, and images

IM: instant message

Text: an electronic message sent over a cellular network from one cell phone to another by typing *words*, often in shortened form, as "l8t" for late

Hash Tags: a way of organizing your Tweets for Twitter search engines; Users simply prefix a message with a community driven *hash tag* to enable others to discover relevant posts like #gobcbclass (go to beyond computer basics classes)

Wall: area on a social website page where friends and "fans" can post their thoughts, views, or attitudes for everyone to see; Walls have three viewing settings: user + others, just the user, and just others

Timeline: section on Facebook where members post their latest comments; Members can also post messages to their friends' Timelines/Walls if their friends allow it

Mobile Devices: small computing device, small enough to be handheld, having a display screen with touch input and/or a miniature keyboard and weighing less than 2 pounds; a smartphone or tablet computer

WORKSHOP 3
JOINING & POSTING TO A SOCIAL NETWORK

USUALLY ANSWERS QUESTIONS SUCH AS
How can I show this spectacular event photo
to all my family and friends?

To post to an online website, usually requires some kind of registration or log in. One of the best things about **Facebook** is that you can see the past, present, and upcoming events **postings** of friends, family, communities or businesses. You can play games like Sudoku or Farmville, where your friends are your neighbors and you help each other out.

You can search for old friends from high school, old jobs, or just someone you lost contact with. Facebook has groups that you can join, and you get to select which groups, friends, and businesses you want to communicate with. Facebook is really big business. When you sign up as a fan of your favorite businesses, you will find coupons, giveaways, and great merchandise deals there for you, too.

Workshop 3   Find Friends Social Networking Practice

Go to **facebook.com**

1. Log into your Facebook account, open a new Facebook
account, or practice posting using our class Facebook page.

2. Send a friend request to: beyond computerbasics.

3. Post a new photo and message to your wall or our class wall.

Step 1. Click in the URL box.

Step 2. Type in facebook.com.

Step 3. Key the requested information in the fill in registration
boxes. Your email address and password will be needed. Fill in
your Profile information.

Step 4. Take a new photo or upload a photo stored on your USB.

Step 5. **Post** a new message such as a message about your
participation in our computer academy workshop classes.

Step 6: Send and receive **friend requests**. You can send a friend
request to our beyond computerbasics Facebook page. Choose
to accept or not to accept **friends** requests. If you want to accept
someone as a friend, **confirm** the friend request.

WORKSHOP 4   VIDEO PRODUCTION
Goal: Produce and Post A Video

Objectives

1. Use video/movie making software.

2. Use creativity to produce a new video.

3. Post a video or video link to a website.

What would be a good video title?

Source: Computer Training Academy OMG Files

WORKSHOP 4   VIDEO PRODUCTION
Produce a New Digital Comic with Free Online Software
Usually answers questions such as how do I make a video?

PRODUCE AN INSTANT COMIC STRIP MOVIE PROJECT 1

Create an instant movie with free Internet software. Dvolver is fun, easy to use, and produces good to great results for a new movie maker.

Let's Practice Making a Dvolver Comic Strip Movie.

1. Go to **dvolver.com.**

2. Click on make a movie.

3. Give your movie a name.

4. Pick a background.

5. Select your plot and characters.

6. Type in what you want each character to say. Try using just a few words.

7. Choose your background music. View and enjoy.

8. *Important*: Bookmark your video site.

9. Go to our Facebook site at beyond computerbasics. Post a new message that includes your dvolver video website link.

WORKSHOP 4   PROJECT 2
CREATING, VIDEO MAKING & POSTING

Answers questions such as how do record my voice on a video?

READ YOUR POEM OR RECORD YOUR SONG AS A VIDEO

Come up with a catchy new song or poetry reading arrangement for our computer academy theme song. Is your arrangement going to be in the style of country, rap, opera, soul, new age, disco, or rock & roll? Yes, feel free to write a new class theme song or a new piece of poetry related to the theme of seniors taking technology/computer classes.

OPEN WORD

STEP 1: Click on the W on the desktop to open Word. Give your poem or song a title and add your name as the author. Use the insert button at the top of the word screen to insert the current date. Key your new poem or song in Word. Save to your USB.

RECORD USING A CELL OR DIGITAL CAMERA AND POST TO FACEBOOK

STEP 2: Ready, set, record yourself, or get another person to record you as you read your poem or sing your song. Be sure to save the recording as a video file. Post your video to our Facebook page at: beyond computerbasics.

WORKSHOP 5   SELLING ONLINE
Goal: Experience selling your craft or other item online

Objectives

1. Discuss online buying and selling tips and safety.

2. Practice selling an item on eBay, Amazon, or Etsy.

jaimeesgreetingcards@yahoo.com

hastytreasures@yahoo.com

gullahgold@yahoo.com

voicespraise@yahoo.com

vegansfriends@yahoo.com

WORKSHOP 5   EBAY ONLINE SELLING
USUALLY ANSWERS QUESTIONS SUCH AS
Will people actually pay good money for this old thing?

One Man's Trash Is Another Man's Treasure
Turning Trash into Treasure on eBay

The largest online market place in the world is **eBay**. Do you make crafts, have stuff People who make crafts really like **etsy.com**. People who write books, or want to sell books like **amazon.com**. The largest marketplace from the old days, or have unused closet purchases that you want to get rid? Vast number of consumers frequent eBay in a single day, an estimated 70 to 100 million.

 To reach these potential buyers, a seller's account or store have to be opened and a PayPal account. First, view a how to sell on eBay video at **youtube.com**.

eBay Selling How-Tos

How To Sell On eBay Step By Step Instructions
Practice—*just practice* registering and setting up a seller's account, for technology learning purposes only

Workshop 5 Online Selling Practice 1

www.ebay.com
- **STEP 1**: Key in **www.ebay.com** and complete registration.
- Name your account based on the type of items that are going to be put up for sale.
- *A telephone number is required.* Go to your email to confirm.

www.paypal.com
- **STEP 2**: Link your eBay account to **Paypal**. Do this in order to get paid or to buy. A bank account routing number and account number is required, or use a card. Suggestion: Use a bank other than a bank where your main money goes. In fact, it may be a good idea to set up a new checking account at a different bank just for eBay stuff.

Note: Both an eBay and a Paypal account have to be set up.

STEP 3: ___*VERY, VERY IMPORTANT*___: Write down your user name and password, immediately, as soon as it is entered and accepted. **Email the user name and password to yourself for both accounts--the eBay account and for PayPal account.**

If you do not enter the right user name and password, the accounts will not open. Write it down and even email it to yourself.

Workshop 5 Online Selling Practice 2

List A Product On eBay.

- **Select a product to list bag** from bags 1-5.

- Practice--**List the product in your bag**. First, go to ebay.com. key in the name of the item in your bag to see if there are similar items like your item already listed? This will clue you in as to how to best list your item. Check during the 7 day auction period to see how bidding is going. Did your item sell?

WORKSHOP 6   PUBLISH
Goal: Author a Useful Document Using Desktop Publishing Programs and/or Websites

Objective

Author a document using Word, Publisher, PowerPoint, and/or an online desktop publishing website.

When will the next 2nd edition be ready?

Preview at: amazon.com

There are still some vendors charging new author thousands of dollars to publish a book or video. However, there are many online websites like Createaspace that can publish your book free of charge.

Workshop 6 Publish Practice 1

Use Createaspace
to Publish A Hard Copy Book or eBook

1. Go to creataspace.com.

2. Create an account.

3. Read and follow publication guidelines.

4. Decide on DVD, ebook, hardcopy, or movie format.

5. Use the already prepared templates for uploading your manuscript and cover file picture(s).

6. When finished, submit files for review. Edit as required.

7. Click on publish.

Workshop 6   Publish   Practice 2
Make A Photo Story Book

What about making a pop-up photo story book for yourself, a child, friend, or just about anyone? There are several web places to do this at no cost to you. These two are easier to use. Some computer experience is needed.

- Our Story - Create a virtual timeline for just about any event. Upload pictures, narrative and/or video.

- Zooburst – Tell your story as a digital 3D pop-up book in a ten or less pages book.

Let's Practice Authoring and Publishing A 3D Popup Book

1. Go to the Youtube how to video entitled, Zooburst 3D Pop Up Books in Augmented Reality at http://www.youtube.com/watch?v=tpmqs7Yn8VU.

Key in this URL or type in the video name.

2. Go to zooburst.com and register.

3. Select 3-D pop-up book.

4. Add text and images/pictures.

5. Publish. View.

WORKSHOP 7   SKYPE
Goal: To Find Out About The Benefits of SKYPE

Objectives
1. To find out how to use SKYPE for free

2. To view an instructional how-to video on using Skype

Computer Academy Graduation
"Skyeable Moment"

You can make a voice or video call to anyone else who also has Skype, anywhere in the world, for free. Find friends and family who are using Skype and add them to your contact list. When you have added them, it's easy to make a call.

Do you want to SKYPE?

Skype is one of the most popular video call services. A lot of equipment is not required. The software is user-friendly, which enables users to make video calls within minutes of downloading it.

If the person you want to talk to also has Skype, it's free to use the service (minus the cost of your Internet connection.) There is a fee if you're calling a regular landline or cell phone, and there's also a cost associated with some of the more advanced services.

Workshop 6   SKYPE   Practice

How To Use SKPE for free

Let's go to this youtube instructional video at:

https://www.youtube.com/watch?v=sAlEWa_lEfl

ABOUT THE AUTHOR

Dr. Canty, a certified Microsoft Office Specialist in Word, is best known for her unique abilities as a highly effective instructional designer, innovator, and professor. This visionary leader specializes in multi-generational curriculum development and teaching.

She collaborates with colleges, universities, and facilities such as senior enrichment centers and housing centers to spread senior citizen computer literacy everywhere—one byte at a time. Student populations include parents, grandparents, care givers, military veterans, inquiring retirees, second career seekers, retired teachers, pastors, civic leaders, and church officers.

SOME SENIOR TECHNOLOGY ACADEMY

PARTICIPANT AFFLIATIONS

Apostolic Community Church PAW, Inc.
Bowens Chapel AME Zion Church
Brunswick County Senior Resource Center
Cape Fear Baptist Church
Cape Fear Community College Continuing Ed.
Columbus County Senior Center, Ransom
Creekwood Housing Education Center
Disabled American Veterans (DAV)
East Columbus Senior Center
Ebenezer Missionary Baptist Church
First Baptist Missionary Church
First Born Holiness Church
Gregory Congregational Church
Johnson Chapel AMEZ Church
Hillcrest Housing Education Center
Lee's Chapel AMEZ Church
Leland Senior Center
Lighthouse Shining Ministries
Leon Mann Enrichment Center
Macedonia Fire Baptized Church
Macedonia Missionary Baptist Church
Moore's Chapel Missionary Baptist
Mt. Calvary Missionary Baptist Church
Mt. Nebo Baptist Church
Mt. Olive AME Church
Mt. Pilgrim Missionary Baptist Church

Shiloh Missionary Baptist Church
Shining Light Ministries
St. Andrews AME Zion Church
St. Luke AME Zion Church
St. Stephens AME Church
Summerville AMEZ Church
Union Missionary Baptist Church
United Senior Citizens Club
United States Air Force
United States Army
United States Civil Service
United States Marine Corps
Veterans Foreign Wars (VFW)
Walter's Chapel AME Zion Church
Williston Alumni Class '62